190

VIỆTNAM

VIỆTNAM

THE

LAND

WE

NEVER

KNEW

.

PHOTOGRAPHY BY GEOFFREY CLIFFORD • TEXT BY JOHN BALABAN

ART DIRECTION BY B. MARTIN PEDERSEN • DESIGN BY JEFF STREEPER

CHRONICLE BOOKS • SAN FRANCISCO

Photography copyright © 1989 by Geoffrey Clifford/Wheeler Pictures
Text and captions copyright © 1989 by John Balaban
Art Direction: B. Martin Pedersen
Design: Jeff Streeper
Vietnam consultant: Greg Kane

Produced by Stephen R. Ettlinger Editorial Projects, New York, NY

Vietnamese folk poetry, © 1980 by John Balaban, used with permission
of Unicorn Press, Greensboro, N.C.
Traditional Vietnamese woodblock prints by Nguyen Tien Chung, from _Littérature
Vietnamienne_, Fleuve Rouge, Hanoi, 1979

Printed in Japan.

Library of Congress Cataloging-in-Publication Data:
Clifford, Geoffrey.
Vietnam: the land we never knew / photography by Geoffrey Clifford;
text by John Balaban.
p. cm.
Bibliography: p.
ISBN 0-87701-597-X — ISBN 0-87701-573-2 (pbk.)
1. Vietnam—Description and travel—1975- 2. Vietnam—Description
and travel—1975- —Views. I. Balaban, John, 1943 - . II. Title.
DS556.39.C56 1989
959.704'4—dc19   89-30683   CIP

Distributed in Canada by
Raincoast Books
112 East 3rd Ave.
Vancouver, B.C.
V5T 1C8
10 9 8 7 6 5 4 3 2 1

Chronicle Books
275 Fifth Street
San Francisco, California 94103

CONTENTS

PREFACE AND ACKNOWLEDGMENTS

I would like to think that my photographs convey emotions as well as information, so rather than try to explain why I returned to Vietnam, I would prefer the images to speak for me. However, it's not that easy. Too many people have already asked "Why go back?" or "Did you find what you wanted?" and "Were the Vietnamese hostile?" as well as other questions that now seem both valid and senseless. I had to go.

My entire wartime tour of duty was spent flying helicopter missions for the United States Army. Whenever I was outside my secured perimeter or airfield, I was airborne, looking down on an incredible landscape. I was too young to be flying those missions, and I was curious about Vietnam. I was never able to wander along Vietnam's back roads, experiencing life as it might be in that country; never able to see, feel, smell, touch, or taste what I wanted; and, most frustratingly, never able to make friends with Vietnamese, to share common feelings in conversation with innocent people. I was an intruder.

Although it did take a long time for me to want to return—or even think about returning—touchdown in Hanoi in 1985 was a more emotional moment than departure from Freedom Hill in Danang in 1972. "Why go back?" How often do we have the chance to go back and try our best to make a positive experience out of a negative one? Vietnam was a trauma that had been lingering inside me for more than a decade. Photography allowed me to return and assemble a body of work that might benefit our understanding. My sincerest wish is that this book, this "work in progress," will aid others with their perceptions of Vietnam and help guide us away from future tragedies.

I must mention those who shared with me the experience of the war. For whatever the reasons we were there, right or wrong, we have a bond that cannot be severed. I am indebted to many veterans over the past twenty years, and, although unable to thank everyone, I have to mention Rudi Csadenyi, Doug Scherer, Peter Forame, Skip Welles, Michael Ives, Phil Eliades, Jim Low, Ted Ehrlich, Joseph Bangert, and Dick Durrance, who have contributed in their very different ways to the spirit of this book.

The Vietnamese have their veterans too. My guide, friend, and interpreter, Nguyen Duc Quang, had spent more than six years fighting for his country along the Ho Chi Minh Trail, without pay, leave, or family contact, and often while alone, scared, or sick with malaria. Traveling day after day with Quang, when sometimes cold rice and a banana were our rations, I grasped his distinction between need and desire, and learned something more about the strength of the Vietnamese. As veterans talking and working together, our exchanges deepened our understanding of each other, of our cultures, and of our common human goals.

I thank the Foreign Press Center in Hanoi for its approval, support, and hospitality throughout this project. Nguyen Quang Dy deserves special mention, although the entire Center took an active interest. And I must mention the efforts of the New York staff of the Vietnamese Mission to the United Nations: over the past four years many of them have helped, and I would like to thank especially Tran Trong Khanh, Pham Duy Thanh, Nguyen Dang Quang, and the current press officer, Ha Huy Thong.

Influenced by the work of Larry Burrows, inspired by Phil Cohen, encouraged by Howard Chapnick, I have many people to thank within the photography profession. I'm grateful that Jan Mason, Jeff Wheelwright, Barbara Baker Burrows, and Peter Howe of *Life* supported this project. But it is so very important for me to point out that this has been a joint effort and that I owe much to my colleagues whose special talents shaped this book: John Balaban, Steve Ettlinger, Marty Pedersen, and Paul Wheeler. There have also been real contributions from friends and co-workers, most notably Sheila Farr, Jeff Streeper, and the staff at Wheeler Pictures. This is our book, and I will forever be indebted to all who contributed.

Most important, I thank my family, which Vietnam has taught me to value even more: my parents, Wynanda and Thomas Clifford, for their support and encouragment; my wife, Penny, for her understanding of my disappearances into Vietnam and for remaining my best friend and critic throughout; and, finally, my son, Stefan, for his compassionate interest in my work. In a very special way, this book is also dedicated to Stefan and his entire generation.

Geoffrey Clifford

For Nanon

INTRODUCTION

For the many millions of Americans who went there, and for the millions who watched on television, Vietnam is the name of a war. Our longest war. Our most troubling war. But a war, even if undeclared. Few of us had any sense of the people, their language, their history, or their beliefs. For many who went there, the landscape was a confusion of crushing heat, monsoons, malaria, bad water, sawgrass, snakes and leeches, where ambushes or booby traps lay waiting in flooded rice paddies, in bamboo thickets along canals and slow muddy rivers, and under the triple canopy of the mountain jungles. But take away the war—*subtract the fear from the landscape*—and it was beautiful, as soldiers often discovered when they were safe and dry and fed, and free, for a moment, to look at another Vietnam.

This book is about that other Vietnam, the one we never knew or only glimpsed. A Vietnam that is three thousand years old, which is tied, as ever, to the growing of rice and to the annual rhythms of the monsoon. A Vietnam that has, over the centuries, gathered cultural momentum from China, from India, and from its own minorities; a Vietnam of the Three Religions—Taoism, Buddhism, and Confucianism—as well as Christianity. A Vietnam that, after centuries of wars against foreign invaders, is

趙嫗逐吳軍

Trieu Au,
Vietnam's Joan
of Arc, riding
her war
elephant into
battle against
the Chinese in
248 A.D.

now struggling to achieve prosperity under its Communist leadership.

You won't find many war photos in this book. The country, of course, is still littered with the war's wreckage—blasted tanks, acres of bulldozed and defoliated forests, moonscapes of bomb craters, airplane graveyards—but these sad reminders can be seen routinely in the portfolios of photojournalists returning from postwar Vietnam. Certainly the physical, psychological, and economic results of "the American war" still distort the life of every Vietnamese, but that is not what Vietnamese dwell on. They look to the future, and, remarkably, they look to the United States for help toward that future.

In his photographs, taken during four trips to Vietnam from 1985 to 1988, Geoffrey Clifford has seen Vietnam as if he were a Vietnamese: with familiar compassion for ordinary people and their doings, with a sense of the magic and grandeur in the landscape, with a sense of human struggle, and with a sense of history.

Clifford did not always feel so open toward Vietnam. For many years after the war, like other veterans, he wanted to "forget the whole damn thing" and get on with his life. He finished college and established himself as a photographer, but eventually he found "the whole thing resurfacing." So, again like many veterans, Clifford began to think of going back to see the place where he had risked his life.

During the war, as a twenty-one-year-old Army lieutenant who had enlisted while in college, he piloted the UH-1, the Huey helicopter, flying combat assaults out of Chu Lai and Danang, ferrying troops and supplies into the war zones. Fourteen years later, on one of the first tour groups to return, he found himself in Hanoi among his former enemies. Since then he has gone back by himself three times. Traveling with his cameras and with Mr. Quang, his expert guide, Clifford is one of the few foreigners *ever* to have traversed the whole length of Vietnam, from the Chinese border in the north to the tip of the Ca Mau peninsula in the south. *Đi ra một ngày, về một sàng khôn*, the proverb says: "Go out one day, come back with a basket full of knowledge."

According to legend, the Vietnamese are the offspring of a dragon, Lac Long Quan, and a mountain spirit or fairy, Au Co. Their union resulted in Au Co's giving birth to one hundred eggs, the "one hundred peoples" of Southeast Asia. Fifty of these children returned with their father to the seacoast; the others remained in the mountains with their mother. Those who went to the sea and to the riverine deltas would become the Vietnamese.

The myth suggests some complex truths. The Vietnamese are indeed related by language and race to many of the Mon-Khmer-speaking peoples of Southeast Asia, of which some sixty groups still live within Vietnam's borders. Some, like the Muong, whose language is basically the same as Vietnamese, are their close country cousins. But thousands of years ago, the Vietnamese left their cousins in the mountains and followed Lac Long Quan, "The Lac Dragon Lord," to the wet-rice delta lowlands where, over the centuries, they absorbed cultural forces coming from China and later, India. These dragon children established an agricultural civilization in the Red and Black River valleys near present-day Hanoi. Thus, the Vietnamese have been living where they are today since the seventh century B.C., when they were known as the Lac and were ruled by kings called Hung, in a country they called Van Lang. In this ancestral domain, they created a sophisticated Bronze Age culture known to archaeologists as Dong-Son.

In 111 B.C. the Chinese completed their conquest of Vietnam. At first the conquest only meant that the Vietnamese, still living under their Lac lords, had to pay tributes and taxes in the form of slaves, forced labor, spices, pearls, kingfishers, rhinoceros horn, and ivory. However, after a failed rebellion led by the Trung sisters in 42 A.D., the Chinese embarked on a harsh direct rule. Ma

Yuan, the Chinese general, had the heads of the Trung sisters sent back to the court at Lo-yang after thousands of rebels were killed in the single, decisive battle at Lang-bac. As the general's armies moved south, unopposed, thousands more were beheaded or deported to China. The Lac dominions were abolished. The Lac Viet were forced to adopt Chinese customs, even Chinese dress. Tay-vu, as Vietnam was then

Vietnamese General Tran Hung Dao, 13th century.

called, disappeared from history and Vietnam was on its way to becoming Annam, "the Pacified South."

The Chinese conquest of Vietnam lasted one thousand years, but those years were not quite as pacified as *Annam* would suggest. At least ten major rebellions occurred from 111 B.C. to 938 A.D., when Ngo Quyen defeated a Chinese armada in the estuary of the Bach Dang River, southeast of Hanoi, and made himself king of

a free Vietnam. Although the Vietnamese were independent for nearly nine hundred

years thereafter, they had to repel Chinese armies again and again throughout the

centuries. The patriotic spirit of Vietnam can be read in the poem (at left) that Ly

Thuong Kiet composed in 1076 to rally his troops against the latest invasion.

The mountains of the South

When the American military entered Indochina on the heels

belong to the Viets of the South.

of the French, we had little awareness of this intense

This is written in the Celestial Book.

nationalism and the degrees of sacrifice that it could arouse in

Those who try to conquer this land

all levels of Vietnamese society. We had little sense of the

Will surely suffer defeat.

military and diplomatic strategies that the Vietnamese had

developed for driving out foreigners. With the Chinese (and, later, with the

French, Japanese, and Americans) the Vietnamese always had to deal with superior

forces. They had to learn how to use the strengths of the enemy to their own

advantage. In 938 A.D., Ngo Quyen knew that he could not meet the Chinese

forces head on; he also knew that their large navy would have to attack his citadel

by sailing up the mouth of the Bach Dang River. He ordered huge timbers (some of which can be seen today in the Museum of History in Hanoi) to be tipped with iron and stuck in the tidal shallows. At high tide these spikes were hidden, and when the Chinese troop ships appeared, the lighter, shallow-drafted Vietnamese boats went out to meet them. The Chinese gave chase as the Vietnamese fled up the Bach Dang, past the submerged timbers, which skewered the Chinese hulls and allowed the Vietnamese to attack and burn the ships.

Sometimes ancient strategies were used against American troops. Early in our war, Vietnamese soldiers used a tactic called "the hawk and the chicken," whereby American helicopters, descending to drop off troops to chase the fleeing Viet Cong, were impaled on bamboo poles too thin to be spotted from the air. Later in the war, General Vo Nguyen Giap, who led Vietnamese forces against American troops, scheduled his surprise Tet Offensive of 1968 on the anniversary of the Tet Offensive of 1789, when yet another Chinese army was defeated by a surprise attack. Vietnamese consciousness is filled with memories of bold tactics that turned the tide of battle. From the Trung sisters to the

南國山河越族居
截然定分在天書
如何逆虜來侵犯
汝等行看取敗虛

Poem by Ly Thuong Kiet, 1076 A.D.

21

French army

taking Hong-

Hua, Tonkin,

August 1884.

twentieth century, Vietnam has raised temples in memory of clever tacticians.

What collective resources have given the Vietnamese the strength to prevail through the centuries and defeat the Chinese? How could technologically backward Vietnam, even with material help from the Soviet Bloc and China, defeat the United States? American soldiers fought well and bravely. Our forces were vastly superior. We dropped more bomb tonnage on tiny Vietnam than fell in all of World War II. So why did they win? Surely some of the factors have to do with the domestic and international constraints placed upon our military operations, but other factors have to do with Vietnamese culture: perhaps it was the millennia of schooling in Taoism, Confucianism, and Buddhism—more than the few decades of Marxism—that provided the Vietnamese with great reserves of clarity and courage in dealing with overwhelming foreign armies.

From Taoism, they learned that "the sword is a cursed thing," that the greatest general is the one least eager to fight, and that power comes from harmony with heaven, with understanding the underlying patterns of things and moving with those patterns. Taoism teaches how to yield, so that the weak can overcome the strong.

Furthermore, a truly strong person doesn't need to show it: *Người khôn ngậm miệng; người mạnh khoanh tay,* "the wise man shuts his mouth; the strong man folds his arms." The proverb is odd for us, commonplace for Vietnamese.

From Buddhism, Vietnamese learned compassion for living creatures, non-attachment to the material world, sacrifice for others, and how to calm and focus the mind. From Confucianism, they learned the importance of history and literature, regard for social order, respect for authority, loyalty to the "five relationships," and the veneration of ancestors, whose spirits, both public and familial, are living presences that guide one's life.

From the Chinese, they borrowed a system of government by which an emperor ruled through a "mandate from heaven," a mandate passed through the centuries from king to king until 1945 when the last emperor, Bao Dai, handed over to Viet Minh officials the Royal Mirror, the *mặt trời* or "face of Heaven," symbol of the right to rule.

The Vietnamese also borrowed from the Chinese some of the very institutions that strengthened them against Chinese invasions. In 1076 A.D., the year that Marshal Kiet drove out the Chinese, he established a Chinese-modeled civil service system, which Vietnamese men of any social class could enter upon passing national examinations. In the same year, the Van Mieu, or the Temple of Literature, was established in Hanoi as a place of study for scholars and prospective administrators. This mandarinate lasted until 1919; for the masses it provided the hope of social mobility through education, and for the court it meant a pool of able leaders not indebted to class or court connections.

King. Scholar. Farmer. Worker. Merchant. Soldier. This is the traditional hierarchy of Vietnamese society. When the French conquest of Indochina ended nine hundred years of independence, that social order was broken. Kings became puppets, sometimes banished to French Africa when they failed to obey their "Protectors General." Mandarins either became colonial lackeys or were kicked out of government.

When the French were finally defeated and the Americans took over in South Vietnam, the social order was turned completely upside down. Soldiers—opportunists of violence, the least-respected social group—became top dogs. Small wonder that our allies, Khanh and Ky and Thieu, won little respect from the southern population. Their only training came from the French army, while the leaders in the north, the older "Marxist mandarins," had been dedicated since childhood to the struggle for independence and steeped in the study of literature and history. "Nothing is more precious than independence and freedom" is the Ho Chi Minh phrase blazoned on banners and placards and engraved on monuments throughout Vietnam today.

Yet postwar Vietnam is not exactly a success. More than ten years after the war, the Communist leadership has not achieved a stable peace or prosperity. The war and its political aftermath have ruined the economy and have placed Vietnam hopelessly in debt: $90 million to the International Monetary Fund, $1 billion to Algeria, Iraq, Libya, and India, and some $5.5 billion to the Soviet Bloc. It is this latter debt, which Vietnam is attempting to pay back with the products of its fishery, farming, and timber industries, that leaves the country in a state almost as desperate as during the Great Depression, when the French plundered the country and thousands starved. In the spring of 1988, Vietnamese leaders appealed to the United Nations for food relief. Starvation

The French governor general of Indochina and the last Vietnamese emperor, Bao Dai, 1934.

L'Illustration

looms again.   Vietnam, once the "rice bowl of Asia," cannot feed itself.

Several factors besides the impoverishing effects of forty years of warfare contribute to Vietnam's troubles. Its old enemy, China, has cut aid and has invaded twice since 1975.   For a decade, Vietnam has maintained 120,000 troops in Cambodia against the Chinese-backed Khmer Rouge under Pol Pot, whose jungle-camp regime was recognized by the United States despite his killing of some two million Cambodian civilians.   Moreover, the U.S. trade embargo, which is also observed by our allies, is still in effect.   Domestically, the Vietnamese leadership, while successful on the battlefield, has floundered in managing the peace: its economic policies, now the subject of sharp internal debate, have actually increased the country's economic difficulties.   But Vietnam's leaders are reaching out for new directions.   Repeatedly, they ask for normalization of relations with the United States as a major step out of their difficulties.

Many Americans want to forget Vietnam.   However, we cannot, must not, forget Vietnam.   We can't because the war is still alive in the memories of the 8,744,000 Americans, men and women, military and civilian, who served there, and the millions

Courtesy John Balaban

Ho Chi Minh reviewing troops removed to North Vietnam following the Geneva Accords, 1957.

more who bore witness to the war at home. We must not forget Vietnam because America, for its moral and political sake, needs to understand what went wrong. We cannot afford to stumble into the next century with the disabilities of an amnesiac.

Clifford's photographs offer a look at a Vietnam we never knew, a Vietnam pursuing a destiny two thousand years in the making. Join him by the seacoasts, in delta villages along slow canals, in crowded cities; take a look at the Vietnamese today, at ordinary people getting haircuts, going to church, summoning ancestors,

walking to school, herding ducks, fishing, weeding rice fields, and sitting around in

conversation, as they are in this turn-of-the-century folk poem, still sung today:

Evening, before the King's pavilion,

people are sitting, fishing, sad and grieving,

loving, in love, remembering, waiting, watching.

Whose boat plies the river mists?

—offering so many rowing songs

that move these mountains and rivers, our Nation.

CHRONOLOGY

2000 B.C.   The north of Vietnam is the center of an extensive Bronze Age civilization, located at Dong Son, south of present-day Hanoi.

700 B.C.   In the plains of the Red and Black rivers, a succession of eighteen Hung kings rule over the Lac Viet, known in ancient Chinese records as the Nan Yueh, or "Southern Viets."

111 B.C.   Chinese conquest of Vietnam. Domination lasts one thousand years despite numerous rebellions.

939 A.D.   Ngo Quyen defeats the Chinese and establishes the first Vietnamese dynasty. Except for brief periods, Vietnam is independent for nearly nine hundred years.

1010   Hanoi, known then as Thang Long, or "Soaring Dragon," becomes the capital of Vietnam. In this century the Vietnamese court establishes the Temple of Literature, the civil service, the One Pillar Pagoda, and the Tran Vu Buddhist Pagoda.

1627   Alexandre de Rhodes, a French Jesuit missionary, writes a grammar of Vietnamese using Roman script, which over the centuries is accepted as the *quốc ngữ*, or "national script." Protection of the missionaries becomes a pretext for repeated French invasions.

1802	Nguyen Dynasty. With the help of both French and Thai armies, Nguyen Anh defeats the populist Tay-Sons.
1858	French troops attack Danang.
1861	Saigon falls to the French.
1883	French consolidate rule over Vietnam.
1945	The last Nguyen emperor, Bao Dai, abdicates in favor of the Viet Minh led by Ho Chi Minh.
1946	French troops shell Haiphong harbor and reenter Hanoi. The Indochina War begins.
1954	French defeated at Dien Bien Phu. Vietnam is temporarily partitioned under the Geneva Accords.
1955	The United States sends military advisors to South Vietnam.
1961	U.S. troops in South Vietnam number 3,200.
1968	Tet Offensive. U.S. troop capacity at 500,000.

1972	The last American ground combat battalion leaves Vietnam on August 23.
1975	Saigon falls to North Vietnamese troops. Vietnam is reunified under the Communist regime in Hanoi. U.S. imposes trade embargo.
1978	The Vietnamese respond to repeated Khmer Rouge incursions in the Mekong Delta by invading Cambodia and driving Pol Pot's troops from Phnom Penh.
1979	China invades North Vietnam with 600,000 troops, which are quickly repulsed. U.S. trade embargo enlarged to include all aid.
1987	Vietnam promises to remove all troops from Cambodia by 1990. President Reagan appoints retired General John W. Vessey, Jr., as a special representative to discuss MIAs (soldiers missing in action) and other humanitarian issues. Movement is begun in Congress to normalize relations with Hanoi.
1988	Joint U.S. and Vietnamese search teams cooperate in locating the remains of missing American soldiers.

RIVERS

AND MOUNTAINS

Nước non is the common phrase for "nation"; it means "rivers and mountains" and suggests how closely Vietnamese identify with their land. *Khi vui non nước cũng vui:* "When man is joyful, the land is joyful." Mountains, rivers, and, of course, the sea are the basic elements that have nurtured Vietnamese society through the millenia as the country shook off foreign domination and expanded southward. As Vietnamese dynasties extended their southern frontiers (subjugating the Champa Kingdom and the Mekong Delta Khmers in the process), Vietnam's borders evolved into the long S-curve that now winds along the coast from the steep mountain passes on the Chinese border to the Ca Mau mangrove swamps jutting into the Gulf of Thailand.

Despite its great length, the land mass is rather small and measures only thirty-one miles at its midsection. Vietnam lies in just one time zone. Three-quarters of the country is mountainous; the rest is coastal plain. The latter is the Vietnamese heartland, for unlike the minority groups, such as the Muong and Black Thai, the Vietnamese seldom live in the mountains. They are a riverine, delta people, prospering beside the big rivers, like the Red River and the Mekong, known as Cuu Long, or "Nine Dragons." Some scholars speculate that the oldest Vietnamese name for themselves, Lac, refers to water. Indeed, it

Preceding page: Summer storm brewing over the Perfume River near Hue. Originally a city of the Cham people, it became a Vietnamese capital of the Nguyen lords in 1687.

is water from rivers and from the annual monsoons that has allowed them to pursue a wet-rice culture far more stable and productive than the dry, upland rice agriculture of the mountain peoples. Working together in hamlets and villages, managing their dikes, ditches, and companionable water buffalo, the Vietnamese have grown to some sixty-two million. Their country, though now impoverished, is rich in arable land, in forests, in fisheries, and in minerals, including recently discovered oil and natural gas along the coastal shelf.

Vietnamese love the land where they have lived for three thousand years, a land for which they have paid in blood many times. The particular quality of that affection is often expressed in fanciful old place names: the Perfume River, the Lake of the Returned Sword, the Pass of Clouds, the Dragon's Jaw Bridge, the Village of Virtuous Teaching, the Temple of the Kneeling Elephant, Ghost Alley. It is a landscape filled with legend.

The earth, rivers, and sea are spiritually alive. Although the proverb tells us that through hard work "an inch of soil can become an inch of gold," the landscape is not just a place of exploit for grinding out a living. Almost every farming home will have a little platform altar just outside the front door for the Soil Spirit. Geomancers are consulted before building a house. Boat prows are painted with eyes for the many water spirits. Certain village trees, usually large banyans, harbor spirits. Spirit houses dot the roadsides.

The visual landscape, especially in the strangely shaped limestone mountains, invites a sense of spiritual presence that Vietnamese often re-create at home in miniature garden grottoes or in the fanciful topiary and bonsai that decorate their yards. Frequently, mountains will have a grotto dedicated to some spiritual entity, often a female, including the Virgin Mary or her counterpart in Buddhism, Quan Om, the Bodhisattva of Mercy. So far, this magical sense of nature has survived modern pressures.

Opposite page:

A rice field with a teapot left for lunch.

Farmers take their lunch in the rice

fields, often eating just some cold rice,

salt, a few greens...and always

bringing along a teapot.

Late afternoon, Ha Long Bay. In boats

not much different than this one, the

Vietnamese have been fishing the bay

since the seventh century B.C.

Beach south of Danang, which during the war was the main hub of American troops in I Corps, the northern zone of South Vietnam. Vietnam has a coastline of some two thousand miles, much of it dazzling beaches. An international resort chain is rumored to have leased beach property just south of Hue.

Fisherman plying
the shoreline
below the
limestone
pinnacles of Ha
Long Bay.

A private home,
fronted with a
topiary island,
on West Lake in
Hanoi. The lake,
once a bend in
the Red River,
was in ancient
times lined with the palaces of the Le
kings and the Trinh lords. Hanoi means
"inside the bend of the river."

Homes on West Lake, Hanoi.

Opposite page: Father and son returning home to Lang Co village, below the Pass of Clouds. As the proverb says, "When young you need your father; when old you need your sons."

The evening meal for this fisherman, docked at Vung Tau, is a bowl of rice with a bit of fish and some vegetables.

Two boys in an ox cart and a man on a bicycle are off to work in the early morning. Few motorized vehicles are available.

A buffalo cart goes past potato fields.

Opposite page: Road to Tay Phuong Pagoda, twenty-five miles southwest of Hanoi.

Typical upland village. This one belongs to the Black Thai minority in Son La province, in the mountains near Laos. Gardens and fruit trees surround houses raised on stilts and hidden behind bamboo fences; chickens and livestock are kept under the decks, where fish and rice are dried.

The French dug many of the Mekong Delta canals early in this century in order to irrigate their vast plantations, to transport their harvests, and to extend their control over the rural villagers. "The French ships run in the new canal" begins a folk poem from the 1930s.

Opposite page: Two homes nestled beneath a limestone mountain in Lang Son province near the Chinese border. The Lang Son passes have been the traditional route of invasion for Chinese armies, including the last incursion in 1979.

Public buses in downtown Hanoi.

A cautious hand extends a firecracker
out a doorway in Hanoi, where the
streets were filled with blasted paper
and smoke during the New Year's
celebration for Tet, 1988.

Opposite page:

Near the old JUSPAO headquarters (Joint United States Public Affairs Office), and City Hall in downtown Ho Chi Minh City. After the war, Saigon was renamed Ho Chi Minh City by the current government.

Catholic church at Lang Co village, near Hai Van, or the Pass of Clouds. On the bay, fishnets are up, ready to be dropped at high tide.

A street corner in Danang, once the capital of the Cham kingdom, which fell to the Vietnamese *nam tiến*, or "march south." Later the Vietnamese themselves were conquered by the French. On March 8, 1965, the first U.S. combat troops landed at Danang.

Opposite page:

Flame trees in flower in Hue.

Lotus pond in Old Hue.

The Reunification Express runs on steam

for the eleven hundred miles from Hanoi

to Ho Chi Minh City.

Cold winter mists

near the Chinese

border.

Above:

A Muong home in the Cuc Phuong forest. The Muong, the upland cousins of the Vietnamese, number some seventy thousand. Ho Chi Minh, who led the Vietnamese against the French, Japanese, and Americans, had a simple Muong-style house built for himself in a park in Hanoi, preferring it to the grand French-built presidential palace.

Below:

Hillside at Khe Sanh, where U.S. Marines held out during the famous seige of the last war. The artillery and bombing were calamitous for the minority tribes living in these mountains; as the proverb says, "When elephants and tigers fight, crickets perish." These girls are carrying stalks that will be made into brooms for export.

A river village in Dong Thap province,

Mekong Delta. The local silts each

produce a distinctive flavor, allowing

Vietnamese to identify where rice was

grown by its fragrance when cooked;

hence, the folk poem:

The Saigon River slides past the Old Market,

its broad waters thick with silt. There,

the rice shoots gather a fragrance,

the fragrance of my country home,

recalling my mother home, arousing deep love.

Washing clothes in the Red River below the new Chuong Duong Bridge.

Villager walking home in the Mekong Delta.

PEOPLE
TODAY

ost of Vietnam's sixty-two million people live in rural villages, not in Hanoi, Hue, or Saigon, the traditional seats of central authority. For these millions of farmers, the *làng*, or communal village, is the focus of their allegiances. Often a farmer's life does not extend beyond the village but is taken up wholly with village customs and with the shared labors of the rice harvest. Growing rice in a monsoon climate is time-consuming and backbreaking. While someday the water buffalo may be replaced by motorized plows, there are aspects of rice growing—like transplanting seedlings one by one in the flooded paddies—that will always require large numbers of people, knee-deep in mucky water, backs bent under the tropical sun, and joined in a task too big for any one family.

Traditionally, the village was an autonomous unit, economically self-sufficient, governed by its own laws and customs, and controlling the use of its communal lands. Its elected village council was charged with settling disputes and with carrying out religious rites associated with each village's Guardian Spirit and founding ancestors, both of which had altars in the village communal house, called the *đình*. Many of these *đình*s—often the most beautiful wooden structure in a village—were destroyed in the first and second Indochina wars. When they still functioned as town meeting halls

Preceding page: Even the weeds from the rice field will be used as food for the family or livestock.

66

and public religious centers, each *đình* contained a document from the king assigning the name of the Guardian Spirit for the village, thus linking it to the royal court. But even in good times, like those expressed in the folk poem below, the villages remained independent and skeptical of outside rule: *phép vua thua lệ làng*, "the King's law yields to village custom." How much, if any, of this old order remains is not certain.

Despite vast social changes caused by wars and revolutions, all Vietnamese still share underlying beliefs created by centuries of Chinese influence, by the many struggles against foreign rule, and, especially, by the subtle promptings of Taoism, Buddhism, and Confucianism. Without any conflicts of piety or ethics, a person can practice all of these religions in one day, depending on how he or she responds to family, to self, to other villagers, to the needy, to field or water spirits, and to ancestors. Throughout the centuries, the "three religions" have intermingled in the popular mind and now form a base for recently acquired belief systems like Catholicism, Marxism, and Cao Dai.

The spiritual thread that binds Vietnamese is tied around family altars, for most Vietnamese homes still maintain altars

When the rice fields lie fallow,

I play the flute lying on the back of my buffalo.

Happy the people with a Thuan-Nghieu king.

Over the land the intelligent mind spreads like the wind.

The Lo waterfalls are clear, free and high.

We shake off the jacket of the dust of life.

to family ancestors, who aren't so much worshipped as consulted and honored. "Birds have nests; men have ancestors" goes the proverb. And just as the nest provides a place of nurture for fledglings, so ancestors provide nurture for the living. Ancestral spirits are asked their advice on any event that may influence the fortune of the family, and they are kept up to date on family affairs. Thus, Confucian obligations of children to parents and of parents to their children continue even after death. In the countryside, the family tombs are set right at the edge of the family rice fields. Vietnamese live close to their relatives, both living and dead.

The biggest spiritual and public event is Tet, often described as Christmas, Thanksgiving, and the Fourth of July rolled up into one holiday. Tet is the annual turning of the lunar year, the start of spring when the whole country, household by household, tidies up, pays off old debts, buys new clothes, prepares special rice cakes, and gets ready for the family reunions that will follow the fireworks on the eve of the new year. Tet is a national ceremony of renewal and hope. At Tet, both the Hearth God, Ong Tao, and the family ancestors depart briefly to report at the Jade Emperor's Heaven as the old year wanes. Of course, they must be sent off and welcomed back with proper ceremonies, including, for those who can afford it, going to market and bringing home a sprig of the yellow-blossomed *mai* tree.

In the wake of a war that destroyed hundreds of thousands of households, killing parents and leaving old people without children to care for them, the ordinary folk in these photographs face a hard life. Many Vietnamese will die of malnutrition in the next few years; many will never find work in a ruined economy. Many have no skills but those of warfare. Still, the main fact of their lives is this: *they are not being bombed.* For the first time in over forty years, Vietnamese can enjoy the marvelous liberty of going out unmolested by air raids and troops, as they get haircuts, go to market or to the beach, tie one on in a local bar, take a noonday nap in a hammock, watch their children run off to play, and "eat Tet" with their loved ones.

For the first time in centuries—despite the undeniable differences that exist between northerners and southerners, between rural and city people—Vietnamese have the chance to shape their future without foreign intervention. Indeed, their long tradition of village independence and popular uprisings suggests that if they do not like their present government, they will change it too.

Two local women rowing home on Ha

Long Bay. Their face masks protect their

lungs from the December chill.

Flower seller near Hanoi.

Near Pleiku, in the Central Highlands, a

Gia Rai man makes a coffee bean sorter.

The Gia Rai, a Malayo-Polynesian group,

number 186,000 and are the largest

minority in the highlands.

Tobacco shop in the coal mining town of

Hon Gai. Packs of cigarettes are piled

on the table, and for those who cannot

afford them, there is a pile of Lao

tobacco, a bamboo waterpipe, and a

kerosene lamp for a lighter. The pig is

just there for a snooze.

Opposite page:

Tourist bus near the Dalat resort.

Burning off rice fields at the end of
harvest in Long An province southwest
of Ho Chi Minh City.

Shenanigans in a Cholon bar. Cholon is

the Chinese district of Ho Chi Minh City.

Many ethnic Chinese left Vietnam after

the Communist takeover.

Afternoon nap in the Dong Thap section
of the Mekong Delta. Almost everyone
takes a siesta.

Child playing
with a 155-mm
artillery casing
near Khe Sanh.

Opposite page:
Street-side barber
shop, Hanoi.

With an extra arrow in his teeth, a Muong hunts birds with a crossbow in the Cuc Phuong Forest.

Opposite page: Woman praying to Buddhist saints at an entrance to the Co Loa temple and ruins. Co Loa citadel, shaped like a snail shell, was the first capital of the Vietnamese in 255 B.C.

Bamboo for sale on a street in Hanoi. Fuel, roofing thatch, walls, room dividers, conical hats, fish weirs, fish traps, and even cowbells and canteens are made from bamboo. Live bamboo hedges surround rural homes.

Flower shop in Hanoi.

Family outing in Ho Chi Minh City. In Hanoi there are few motorcycles—fewer still in private hands—and gasoline is scarce.

Tet balloons.

Street vendor in Ho Chi Minh City reading Erich Segal's *Love Story*. A time warp exists here, where 1960s rock-and-roll and paperbacks are still recycled.

Opposite page:
Tai chi by the Saigon River. One commonly sees quiet, unsupervised groups of young and old practicing slow, rhythmic tai chi exercises early each morning in the public parks.

Quan Su Pagoda. The "Ambassadors' Pagoda" was built in the fifteenth century for diplomats from the neighboring Buddhist countries of Laos and Siam. It is the most

active Buddhist center in Hanoi. Here a man prays for the soul of a relative whose picture joins others on the communal altar.

Temple on top of Marble Mountain,

south of Danang. During the last war, a

Viet Cong medical unit was stationed in

caverns deep inside the mountain; a

U.S. airfield was nearby.

Catholic church at
the foot of
limestone
mountains in Ha
Nam Ninh
province, south of
Hanoi.

Hanoi Deputy Bishop Nguyen Van

Sang and Cardinal Trinh Van Can.

Vietnam has about three million

Catholics.

Quan Om, the Bodhisattva of Mercy, at Co Loa Temple, near Hanoi. Vietnam has been a Buddhist country for nearly two thousand years.

Opposite page: Main hall, Cao Dai Temple, Tay Ninh. Cao Daism, which may have nearly two million advocates, was founded in 1919 by Ngo Van Chieu, receiver of the Third Revelation. Under French and Japanese control, the sect kept its own army. It is as warily regarded by the current regime as it was by the previous one.

Guide at the Cao Dai Temple in Tay Ninh. Cao Daism, which has a number of branches, is an eclectic, all-unifying faith whose dieties include Christ, Buddha, Winston Churchill, and Victor Hugo.

Man on the Mekong ferry to Can Tho.

Nha Trang beach.

Ba Da Pagoda, Hanoi. The woman

has a prayer book for the Amitabha

Buddha, the "Buddha of the Western

Peace," the main devotional figure in

the largest branch of Mahayana

Buddhism in East Asia: Pure Land

Buddhism.

Crowded food stalls in the main

market in Ho Chi Minh City, formerly

Saigon, where the stalled economy

accrues its sharpest discontent. The

sign says simply, "Eat and drink."

Karate class, Hue.

Fish market at Bang Lat village,

southwest of Hue.

A girl studies while taking a pedicab to

school in Nha Trang. The scene is much the

same as pre-1975, but her lesson book, with

Lenin on the back cover, represents a new

regimen for South Vietnamese children.

HEAVENLY

MANDATE, EARTHLY RULE

The ancientness of Vietnamese history gives the people a sense of identity that feeds their national pride and independence. When they consider monuments as old as the Co Loa citadel, built two centuries before the Christian era, they have a mark against which all their contemporary affairs are measured. They know that the major dynasties of their past were established by generals, at the head of irregular peasant armies; that the early kings were described as *bố cái đại vương,* "great father/mother kings," because they were especially close to the people. Similarly, departed national heros, like General Tran Hung Dao, are sometimes thought to guide the nation from their temples and tombs as *thánh,* spirit-saints. Ho Chi Minh's mausoleum can be better understood in this sense than as the Stalinesque crypt described by journalists.

After they adopted the nomenclature of the Chinese court, the Vietnamese kings were described as holding a "mandate from heaven," a favoring from the heavenly powers that gave their rule legitimacy. When at times these rulers became inept at governing, the common people looked for some bold figure—often from the peasantry—to bring about a "change of season," a revolution that would establish a new heavenly agreement. The guerilla armies that rose up behind such leaders have often swept through Vietnamese

Preceding page: The National Assembly at its 1987 meeting, during which it voted in the current reformist regime.

history, overturning domestic rulers as well as foreign. So it was out of healthy respect for popular sentiment that in 1945 the Viet Minh were careful to have the last holder of the heavenly mandate, Emperor Bao Dai, turn over his royal insignia in a special ceremony.

The Marxist leaders of contemporary Vietnam feel an accountability that may surprise outsiders. General Secretary Linh and his fellow reformers know they must satisfy deep popular aspirations and discontents. "If I don't deliver," he told Clifford in their photo session, "I'll be out." In fact, Mr. Linh and his reformist colleagues are in power now because the older, more doctrinaire leadership that had successfully managed the war proved unable to manage the peace. Vietnam is in economic ruins. Its current leaders, whatever mandate they hold, must find a way out of the costly war in Cambodia; they must come to some agreement with their traditional enemy, China; and they must get the economy going so that their war-weary population can at last achieve some measure of prosperity.

Almost all recent American visitors to Vietnam—but veterans especially—have been stunned by the lack of rancor and even by the friendliness of Vietnamese. Repeatedly, Vietnamese say, "We do not blame you but the government that sent you here to fight." Certainly the Vietnamese are pragmatists and see no purchase in offending Americans now:

a small nation cannot afford grudges. After almost all their major defeats of the Chinese, the Vietnamese quickly initiated diplomatic missions offering tribute and respects to the Chinese court. But while this may be wise politics, expected from clever diplomats, American visitors find no animosity even in chance meetings with common people. Perhaps the reason lies in the Vietnamese notion of revolution as "change of season." In other words, the "American war" is history. What's done is done. Like the annual lunar cycle that sweeps away all the troubles of the past year at Tet, a revolution offers new possibilities.

There are other reasons for this friendliness to Americans. Some are clearly pragmatic: to move the economy, Vietnam needs a lifting of the U.S. trade embargo. But other reasons have to do with ideals close to American hearts, for the Communist founders of modern Vietnam looked to the United States as a model. In 1945, when writing Vietnam's constitution, Ho Chi Minh paraphrased the American Declaration of Independence.

Boys playing soccer before an old imperial memorial by the Perfume River in Hue. The earlier inscription has been replaced by the Ho Chi Minh quote that became a motto for the revolution: "Nothing is more precious than independence and freedom."

General Tran Hung Dao's effigy in his temple in Hanoi. In the thirteenth century, the general defeated an invading Mongol army of five hundred thousand and ever since has been venerated throughout Vietnam.

Opposite page: Cham ruins. Once a powerful Hindu kingdom in central Vietnam, Champa clashed repeatedly with the Vietnamese and disappeared as a kingdom in the fifteenth century, although the Chams remain a large minority in Vietnam and Cambodia.

Vo Nguyen Giap. General Giap directed the wars against the French and Americans. A history teacher who escaped French arrest by fleeing to China, Giap met Ho Chi Minh there in 1940. Giap was the strategist of the battles for Dien Bien Phu and Khe Sanh, as well as the Tet Offensive.

Retired Prime Minister Pham Van Dong. His lifelong friends, Ho Chi Minh and Vo Nguyen Giap, together with Dong, formed the "iron triangle" that defeated Japanese, French, and American troops. Ho Chi Minh referred to Dong as "my other self."

Morning exercises at a naval unit along the Saigon River in Ho Chi Minh City.

Soldiers on a Hungarian motorcycle near the Chinese border. In just one month in 1979, six hundred thousand Chinese troops crossed the border before being driven back.

East German housing construction in Hanoi. Shoddy as this may seem, it is a step toward accommodating the many residents whose present homes lack sewage and running water. During the last forty years of warfare in the North, almost no large-scale housing projects were begun.

Scholar rolls, Temple of Literature, Hanoi. In 1070, Emperor Ly Thanh Tong ordered the creation of the Van Mieu, where young Confucian scholars would be trained for the civil service. From 1484 to 1788, the names of exam winners were engraved on stone stelae.

Artillery battery at Lang Son on the Chinese border. Maintaining a regular army in Cambodia and a large militia here, where sporadic clashes continue, adds a further drain on Vietnam's economy and the endurance of its people, weary of war.

At an artillery base in Lang Son near the Chinese border, site of recent clashes between the Chinese and Vietnamese.

Nguyen Van Linh,

the current

general secretary

of the Communist

Party. A southerner by birth, Mr. Linh is

a pragmatist charged with achieving

economic and social reforms.

Opposite page:

Inside the National Assembly in Hanoi.

Ho Chi Minh's tomb, where the leader lies embalmed and under glass. He died in 1969 at the age of seventy-nine.

In silence, an honor guard escorts visitors to Ho Chi Minh's tomb.

Ho Chi Minh is venerated like the revolutionary leaders of the past. Since his death, and with the retirements of Pham Van Dong, Vo Nguyen Giap, and others from the original old guard of the Indochina Communist Party, no national figure has emerged to lead Vietnam in peacetime.

SACRIFICE

The war's human sacrifice was immense for the Vietnamese. South Vietnamese troop casualties were nearly 185,528; North Vietnamese and Viet Cong losses were 924,048, with well over 100,000 missing in action. Even more staggering is the number of civilians killed, estimated by the U.S. Subcommittee to Investigate Problems Connected with Refugees and Escapees at more than the total combatant deaths of either side. Because this was a war without front lines, most of the civilians were killed in village cross fires or in the relentless bombings, whose tonnage was four times that dropped in all of World War II. Most civilian casualties were women, or children under 16 years of age—those least able to flee the mayhem. Vietnam is stalked by ghosts, "wandering souls" in popular belief.

Beyond this loss of life, the survivors—the shell-shocked, the widows, the orphans, the drug addicts, the prostitutes, and the millions of men whose only skills are in killing—must bear tremendous psychological burdens.

As if these burdens were not enough, the war continues to devastate two groups long after the last North Vietnamese Army tanks rolled into Saigon. These are the victims of Agent Orange, and the amputees, an estimated sixty thousand of whom survived the war. These amputees are largely our former South Vietnamese allies who lost their limbs while sweeping

Preceding page: Child at a graveyard along the Ho Chi Minh Trail. The dead are arranged according to the provinces that they came from.

for the enemy. In the North, the air war usually obliterated its victims.

The Agent Orange syndrome, which afflicts thousands of American veterans, is of course magnified in Vietnam, where dioxin residues still persist in the food chain and where malformed infants and livestock continue to be born at an unusual rate. Most of these Agent Orange babies are stillborn. With no means to treat or even predict the problem, Vietnamese doctors simply preserve fetuses for further study. They are hoping that American scientists will come to Vietnam for cooperative research that they believe will benefit both countries.

Such humanitarian concerns may provide the first bridges between the two countries since the war. A recent diplomatic mission, led by retired General John W. Vessey, Jr., opened the possibility that the United States will offer some help in establishing prosthetic rehabilitation centers for amputees in return for greater Vietnamese assistance in locating the remains of the 2,483 Americans still listed as missing in Vietnam, Cambodia, and Laos.

Many Vietnamese must wonder if their victory and postwar peace—stalked by hunger and poverty, and ravaged by the results of the fighting—are worth their huge sacrifices. Nonetheless, they are alive, their nation is theirs once again, and their children will be able to grow up to answer that question.

Vo Thi Lien and her daughter, Lien Anh. Mrs. Lien was eleven at the time of the massacre of the village of Co Luy, or My Lai 2. She and her grandfather were the only survivors. She lost thirty-four relatives. Now she works at a museum in Danang.

Bomb crater, now a rice paddy, along Route 2, near the former Demilitarized Zone (DMZ). A local farmer said, "Well, there's no reason we have to have *square* rice fields." Across the stream is an old French bunker.

Trinh Cong Son wrote protest songs popular in South Vietnam during the war.

Pham Thi Trinh, survivor of the My Lai Massacre, standing before the monument raised to the 504 civilians slaughtered by Lt. William Calley and his soldiers as they swept through the My Lai village complex, which contained no enemy soldiers. Miss Trinh, who was eight at the time, survived by crawling under the bodies of her parents. She is the only survivor out of 11 in her family.

Madame Thu Huong, or "Hanoi Hannah,"

as she was known to G.I.s for her radio

broadcasts of propaganda.

A very old Le Cham (109) and his middle-aged son (46), Le Xuan Thong, walk the Ho Chi Minh Trail near Khe Sanh. Mr. Cham helped build the road as far as Khe Sanh during the "French" war. Later, he was captured and tortured by Diem police; afterwards he fled to Hanoi. His son fought against the Americans here in 1968 and is now vice president of the local People's Committee.

Country barber-shop, outskirts of Hanoi.

B-52 crash site. Most war relics have been removed, but some have been left untouched because they are too large to move, or, like this plane, they serve as war sculpture and stir the public

memory. Other sites are preserved because they may contain clues or remains of missing U.S. servicemen; nearly nineteen hundred Americans are still listed as missing in Vietnam.

A bridge still unrepaired from American bombing.

An American tank lies abandoned by the roadside of Highway 1, near Dong Ha.

Opposite page: Years of hardship show on the face of this man, who invited Clifford into his house in Hue. His family was holding a *giỗ đầu,* a ceremony for the first anniversary of a relative's death.

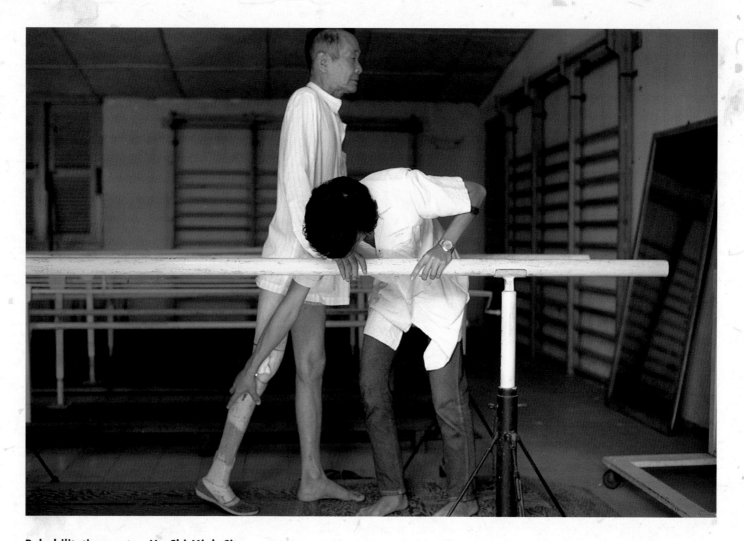

Rehabilitation center, Ho Chi Minh City.

Most of the estimated sixty thousand

amputees are in the south.

Nursery, Tu Du Hospital, Ho Chi Minh City. The war left a public health burden too large and complex for Vietnam to address adequately: infants deformed from Agent Orange and thousands of civilian and military amputees.

HOPE

FOR THE FUTURE

The poorest Vietnamese sometimes refer to themselves as *bụi đời*, "dust of life," blown about in the Buddhist sense by worldly forces, their fortunes almost always in the hands of others. For most of this century, Vietnam has been *bui đời*. Now, with independence, it has a chance to shape its own destiny. It must do so with few capital resources and with a huge international debt. Essentially, the Vietnamese must exploit their country's material resources with the same means used a thousand years ago: *the people*, the sixty-two million ordinary folk who offer vast reserves of will and manpower. Like the boy off to tackle a field with a hoe, Vietnam is struggling for prosperity with simple technology. Instead of handy Japanese irrigation pumps, paddy tillers, threshers, and dryers, the land will be worked by men, women, children, and water buffalo. The rice sheaves will be brought in by ox cart and whacked into bins by hand. The fields will be gleaned for the last grain.

Nothing is thrown away in postwar Vietnam. Colonial-era Citroëns still weave through the cities along with the remnants of the U.S. Embassy motor pool, while old John Deere tractor engines often supply the power for boats plying the Mekong. The country hungers for the technological tools to create prosperity.

Preceding page:

Threshing rice.

The future of Vietnam will be difficult as long as several political problems remain unresolved. Foremost is the U.S. trade embargo. If it were lifted, Vietnamese could trade with the West and Japan as well as receive credit and economic assistance from the United States and from our allies, who also observe the embargo. To lift the embargo, Vietnam must first extricate itself from Cambodia, where it is already reducing troops but where it fears the return of Pol Pot's Khmer Rouge once its occupying army is removed. To settle this problem, Vietnam must settle its difficulties with its ancient enemy and sometime ally, China, which supports the Khmer Rouge. Furthermore, Vietnam's problems with China include the disputed sovereignty of the potentially oil-rich strings of islands known in the West as the Spratleys and the Paracels. Finally, before the United States will establish diplomatic relations with Vietnam, it wants Vietnam to provide greater help in locating the remains of MIAs. None of these objectives is impossible, and with a more open regime in Hanoi, with the atmospheric changes caused by *glasnost*, and with genuine interest stirring in the United States, movement has begun on these issues.

In this country, progress toward normalization of relations is being led by John

McCain, Republican Senator from Arizona. Son and grandson of U.S. admirals,

McCain spent five and one-half years as a prisoner of war in Hanoi after his Navy jet

was shot down and he suffered a broken leg and two broken arms. In 1988, McCain

introduced legislation to begin normalization of relations with his former captors. In

May of that year, he was quoted in the *New York Times* as saying he had "no particular

affection for the Vietnamese," but that "I'd like to make it clear that I hold no hatred

either. I don't think that's a productive enterprise." He added, "It cannot harm the

situation in any way to establish a permanent dialogue" with Hanoi.

Vietnamese authorities want that dialogue. Without normalization of diplomatic

relations and the lifting of economic sanctions, the future for Vietnam is bleak. When

Geoffrey Clifford was photographing leaders in Vietnam, he showed Pham Van Dong,

the former prime minister, some of these photographs. Clifford asked Mr. Dong, who

directed Vietnam's affairs for the last thirty years, if he would offer a comment for the

readers of this book. Months later, Mr. Dong sent this response:

"Dear American Friends,

I invite you to a journey into this collection of photographs. Look carefully and a stirring silent dialogue is likely to weave itself between yourselves and these photographs. A dialogue which goes the way of our contemporary world.

As for myself, in so far as I appear in these photographs, mine will be the gladness of meeting a myriad of Americans from all walks of life, men and women, old and young, at home and out on the roads or streets of the city or the countryside, across the vast expanse of your richly diverse land. And to them I shall tell a tale of friendship and mutual understanding, of the multi-faceted ties that link both our peoples, the Vietnamese and the American peoples."

Harvesting rice near
Long Xuyen in the
Mekong Delta.

Opposite page:

Hanoi Conservatory. A picture of Villa
Lobos is on the wall.

IMEXCO seafood

export company in

Ho Chi Minh City.

Opposite page:

Soviet ships docked in Ho Chi Minh City.

With the U.S. trade embargo, most of

Vietnam's trade is with the Eastern Bloc.

Black Thai family. Peace has brought the greatest benefits to rural people, both Vietnamese and minorities, who have resumed farming and family life close to the earth. Four generations of the family live under the same roof.

Opposite page: Cigarette stand in Ca Mau. Behind the hammock the billboard reads, "Do everything for our children."

Ballet studio,

Hanoi. Ballet is

one of the areas,

like music and math, in which young

Vietnamese are beginning to receive

international recognition.

Mining a cliff face under a moon. As the folk poem says: "As long as there's a sky, rivers, and mountains/ and wind and moon, there's joy for man."

Opposite page: Patches upon patches. From an early age, farmers struggle to feed themselves with the simplest technology in a land neglected and damaged by the war.

Dredging seashells for road repairs.

Cotton worker making quilts for the cold winters.

Schoolboy with
his Young
Pioneer scarf
tucked in his
pocket.

Citroën from the
French era. With
so few resources,
nothing is
thrown away.

Drying rice on the
road near Dalat.
The road is being
used for want of
a clean, flat, dry
place.

Tarring a road.

Opposite page:
Bringing in the
sheaves near Tay
Ninh.

Two boys from Haiphong. Their generation is the first in fifty years to be born during peacetime.

Former soldier Joseph Bangert with Mr. Khanh, whose unit fought against Bangert's during the war.

Opposite page:

Nha Trang beach.

Bus in Dalat. "Go out and see the sun's face, and the moon's," encourages a folk poem.

West Lake, Hanoi.

FOR FURTHER REFERENCE

John Balaban, *Ca Dao Vietnam: A Bilingual Anthology of Vietnamese Folk Poetry* (Greensboro: Unicorn Press, 1980).

John S. Bowman, ed., *The Vietnam War Almanac* (New York: World Almanac Publications–Bison Books, 1985).

Joseph Buttinger, *The Smaller Dragon* (New York: Praeger, 1958).

Frances Fitzgerald, *Fire in the Lake* (Boston: Atlantic–Little, Brown, 1972).

Gerald Hickey, *Village in Vietnam* (New Haven: Yale University Press, 1964).

Gerald Hickey, *Sons of the Mountains: Ethnohistory of the Vietnamese Central Highlands to 1954* (New Haven: Yale University Press, 1982).

Stanley Karnow, *Vietnam: A History* (New York: Viking, 1983).

David G. Marr, *Vietnamese Anti-Colonialism: 1885–1925* (Berkeley: University of California Press, 1971).

John T. McAllister, Jr., and Paul Mus, *The Vietnamese and Their Revolution* (New York: Harper & Row, 1970).

Nguyen Khac Vien, *Tradition and Revolution in Vietnam* (Washington: Indochina Resource Center, 1975).

Ralph Smith, *Vietnam and the West* (Ithaca: Cornell University Press, 1971).

Keith Weller Taylor, *The Birth of Vietnam* (Berkeley: University of California Press, 1983).

Truong Buu Lam, *Patterns of Vietnamese Response to Foreign Intervention, 1858–1900*, Southeast Asia Monograph Series No. 11 (New Haven: Yale University Southeast Asia Studies, 1967).

Danny J. Whitfield, *Historical and Cultural Dictionary of Vietnam*, Historical and Cultural Dictionaries of Asia, No. 7 (Metuchen, N.J.: The Scarecrow Press, 1976).

Alexander Woodside, *Vietnam and the Chinese Model* (Cambridge: Harvard University Press, 1971).